Come Egypt

Poetry by

Teresa E. Gallion

Inner Child Press, ltd.

Credits

Author
Teresa E. Gallion

Editor
Debbi Brody

Foreword
Mary Dezember

Cover Design
inner child press, ltd.

General Information

Come Egypt

Teresa E. Gallion

1st Edition: 2024

This Publishing is protected under the Copyright Law as a "Collection". All rights for all submissions are retained by the individual author and / or artist. No part of this publishing may be reproduced, transferred in any manner without the prior **WRITTEN CONSENT** of the "Material Owner" or its representative, Inner Child Press International. Any such violation infringes upon the Creative and Intellectual Property of the Owner pursuant to International and Federal Copyright Law. Any queries pertaining to this "Collection" should be addressed to the Publisher of Record.

Publisher Information:
Inner Child Press International
www.innerchildpress.com

This Collection is protected under U.S. and International Copyright Laws.

Copyright © 2024: Teresa E. Gallion

ISBN-13: 978-1-961498-17-4 (inner child press, ltd.)

$ 14.95

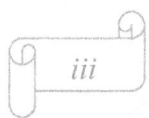

Dedication

To The Memory of

Hertzog And Teresa Lewis Gallion

Two Loving Parents

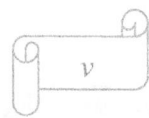

Table of Contents

Foreword   xi

Preface   xv

Acknowledgments   xvii

Captured Moments

Come Egypt	5
Egyptian Yacht	10
Brief Exposure	11
Goddess of Protection	12
Egyptian Moment	13
King and I	14
Nubian Prince	15
Horse and Buggy Ride	16
Goddess in the Sahara	17
Homage to Aida Dehabeya	18

Shapeshifting Between Time and Space

Reserved Space	21
Mount Nebo Reflections	22

Table of Contents ... *continued*

Against the Sun	23
The River Still Flows	24
Ancient Sightings	27
Hieroglyphics and Butterscotch	29
Water Lyrics	30
River Fantasy	31
Waking Dream	32
Pathway to Growth	33
Abu Simbel Intrusion	34
Woman of Value	36
Egyptian Portal	37

Musings on the Nile River

Words to Love You	41
Scream into the Silence	43
Waiting for You	44
Soul Upheaval	45
Catch the Wave	46

Table of Contents ... *continued*

Law of Silence	47
Lyrical Release	48
Soar Like an Eagle	49
Never Alone Again	50
Redemption	51

Temple Hopping – Tomb Walking

My Womb	55
Dear Nefertari	57
What Bodies	59
Key of Life	60
Dancing in the Valley of the Kings	61
Letter to Tutankhamun	63
Hatshepsut	64
It Was a Lie	65
Goddess Isis Speaks	66
Descendant Ones	67
Behold Me	69

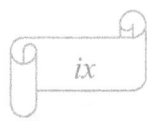

Table of Contents ... *continued*

Ancient Myths of the Gods	70
Wall Paintings	71
Inhale and Exhale	72
Hallelujah Egypt	73

Epilogue

About the Author	77
About Mary Dezember	79
What People are Saying	81
Other Works by the Author	91

Foreword

If you've ever made a wish that you knew the magic words that might transport you in time and space, then open Teresa E. Gallion's *Come Egypt* for a wish come true.

These are poems spun with magic, elevating your reading moment into a spectacle of awareness arisen from the depths of ancient memories.

The poet Teresa E. conjures the mysterious remembering as stunning images, word craft, and ecstatic substance.

The happening of *Come Egypt* is being spread across the eras by the river of time, mainly in Egypt, but also in the place where all rivers connect.

Time and space conflate as historical Egypt and the poet's homeland of contemporary New Mexico juxtapose then converge as the Nile, Rio Grande, and Arkansas Rivers join in her poetry.

Each poem is as smooth and masterful as the speech of ancient goddesses. Here are just a few of Teresa E.'s extraordinary lines in *Come Egypt*:

> "I am a goddess with angel wings/shaking sand off my feathers/as I rise./Licking the

sand/from my hands. Time is calling." (from "Come Egypt")

"Rose petals etched with the names/of beloveds rise from the sand." (from "Come Egypt")

"When evening bends the light rays/across the river, the water whispers/just beneath the surface." (from "Come Egypt")

"The river sings an ode to joy/through the millennia." (from "Come Egypt")

"The ecstasy makes me float like a goddess." (From "Egyptian Yacht")

"A frost-bitten wind/staggers to sleep." (from "Brief Exposure")

"In the Sahara my soul swims/in ancient red sand." (from "Goddess in the Sahara")

Passage on the spectacular yacht Aida, a recurring theme, is simultaneously a passage on the physical rivers and the spiritual rivers.

This collection is arranged as a journey of four parts.

In the first section, experience with the poet the exquisite shock of coming home to a place never before visited.

Immediately taken to an otherworldly realm, we are reminded that the spiritual is the eternal fantastic backdrop for any contemporary day—that of everyday life.

Throughout this section, the poet is drawn to a once-forgotten extraordinary time while ordinary life happens all around her: "We want to see the magnificence/of temples rising from the sand./The intrigue of nature's power/to hold beauty and stories/after a few thousand treks around the sun./The locals speed past in variable/modes of transport doing their daily tasks." (from "Horse and Buggy Ride")

The second section moves to the arrival back to that once-forgotten time and a reckoning of that past with lyrics singing a confident, poised soulful self who orders time, such as "Woman of Value" and "Egyptian Portal."

In the third section, the poet settles into multiple lifetimes, calling to a lover of myriad incarnations with poetry of passionate intensity, such as "Scream Into the Silence" and "Soul Upheaval."

By the fourth section, the poet, now enriched through enchanted travel, returns to the scene of rulers and goddesses, speaking to them or *as* them.

Circular in its quest of discovery-exhilaration-revelation, the collection begins with the poem "Come Egypt" and ends with the poem "Hallelujah Egypt."

I read the poetry of this book as incantations invoking goddesses flowing as river muses of mysticism that surround us while contemporary goddesses, often disguised as poets, walk among us.

Step into the river vessel of *Come Egypt* to travel the transcendent worlds beautifully crafted by Teresa E. Gallion. This is a trip you will want to take—and lives you will want to live—again and again.

Read, then feel the happening.

Mary Dezember, Ph.D.

Preface

The journey to Egypt was a life changing experience. Flashbacks floating down the Nile River embraced me with memories bubbling in the solitude of a river's flow. With each day I was caught in the moment of a revelation of connection through time and space. My muse challenged me to capture my visions and wrap words around what I was seeing, feeling, hearing throughout the landscape that tickled and teased my soul. I felt a wave of redemption bathe my soul in the light of humility and the blessing of an eagle's vision.

This collection rides on the waves of past lives that grabbed me in the reverent walks through the temples and tombs of a regal civilization and my connection to that landscape and people of that era. This was a growth opportunity on my personal journey into a window of time. The stories on the walls gave me lights of understanding to move my learning curve forward. The recognition that every encounter is an opportunity to expand our consciousness is a gift. Enlightenment comes in subtle ways. Every breath, every step, every thought, every utterance from the temple and tomb walls sent messages to me at every moment I was ready to receive the voice of ancient tongues.

I float in gratitude for the exposure to this ancient history that weighed heavily on my heart strings. I felt the load of a civilization rising from the sand in my dreams and meditations across a two-week time span of now that floated back 4000 plus years. My muse is still singing and dancing to the unveiled lyrics of ancient Egypt. The power of Spirit to call us out is available to all souls. Each of us is a messenger and a seeker on different pathways to our destination. Our experiences and reactions are individually different. Those differences are tools for learning and growth when we embrace the writing of others. May you be moved by the intensity of my time travel shapeshifting between the land of Egypt and my beloved New Mexico home.

I pay homage to the eleven souls and our tour guide who shared this journey with me and the everlasting bond we made in the heat of the Egyptian Desert and the royal comfort of our Egyptian yacht. Each one of us assimilated knowledge in our own personal way. But the laughter we shared and the moments of awesome recognition of the power of what we saw melded our energy in positive memories.

Teresa E. Gallion

Blessings
February 2024

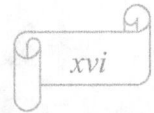

Acknowledgments

Grateful acknowledgement is made to the following Anthologies in which many of these poems first appeared:

Year of the Poet Monthly Anthologies 2022 and 2023.

TESORO 1st Anniversary Firesingers, 2023

As always, a special thank you to Debbi Brody who keeps me grounded in editing my work and has supported my work for many years. Thank you for your loving kindness.

A special thank you to Mary Dezember, Kim Ports Parsons and Michael Anthony Ingram for your loving support and kindness in reading this body of work.

A special thank you to Kim Bromley who shared the two-week journey through Egypt with ten other travelers and our tour guide. Our permanent bond on the Aida Dehabeya shall remain with us forever. Habibi.

Cover art by nirbheek on Fiverr

Come Egypt

Poetry by

Teresa E. Gallion

Teresa E. Gallion

Captured Moments

In that moment
The window of time
Opened its door
And invited me to enter

Come Egypt

Teresa E. Gallion

Come Egypt

All my dreams spill over the waterfall.
I watch the blossoms stream down.
I see the tombs of gods, goddesses and pharaohs
beckoning my soul to come home.
I hear singing in the wind.

Come Egypt! Come home!

I left no trace of the last trail
I took before translation.
Here I stand today
with flutters in my ears.

Come Egypt! Come home!

I tiptoe in the Egyptian desert.
Gently rest my boots on the ground.
Bow my head with respect and awe
to the wondrous carvings
from the sand calling my name.

Come Egypt! Come home!

I am a goddess with angel wings
shaking sand off my feathers
as I rise. Licking the sand
from my hands. Time is calling.

Come Egypt! Come home!

I have trekked around the sun
four thousand times plus one

Come Egypt

and I hear a voice messaging my soul.
Come Egypt! Come home!

Nubians dance with an urgency
that grabs my attention.
Drums of harmony play
a homecoming ritual in my name.
Shouting out loud.

Come Egypt! Come home!

I walk in the tomb of Rameses III
and the hieroglyphics pull at my heart.
Resistance is not an option
when the stimulus is so strong.

Come Egypt! Come home!

Your mummy is no longer usable.
It crumbles in the atmosphere.
You must embrace a new body to bind your soul.

Come Egypt! Come home!

Cloud clusters cry in my name
flow into my river of radiance.
Drenched in your tears, my heart
melts in a wave of love.

Come Egypt! Come home!

The river sings an ode to joy
through the millennia.
Here we stand on the deck
of an Egyptian yacht listening.

Teresa E. Gallion

Come Egypt! Come home!
Inhale the wind of the morning river.
Fold arms around the warmth of hoodies.
The morning chill calls the morning brew
to assist the sunrise in song.

Come Egypt! Come home!

Gratitude floats on the deck of Aida
for the blessing of this ancient experience.
Solitude opens its wings to first light
and the delight of the river's flow.
The sound current streams.

Come Egypt! Come Home!

The first sighting of morning
a water buffalo stands
at the edge of the river staring.
Slowly chewing its morning mulch,
I can feel the song in its heart.

Come Egypt! Come home!

Rose petals etched with the names
of beloveds rise from the sand.
I cannot get you out of my dreams.
Walking meditations along the Nile River.
Vibrations in the breeze enfold me.

Come Egypt! Come home!

When evening bends the light rays
across the river, the water whispers
just beneath the surface.

Come Egypt

Come Egypt! Come home!

The river's musical surge
makes me breathe deep in my soul.
My ears twinkle like stars overflowing
with energy. I hear.

Come Egypt! Come home!

I bow in reverence at the water's edge.
A blanket of earth supports this river
as it stumbles over words to spell grace.

Come Egypt! Come home!

A colored girl's muse rises from its ashes,
flies above the river and speaks
in the tongue of the goddess.

Come Egypt! Come home!

She opens her mouth wide.
The breakfast of her tongue
sings without resistance.

Come Egypt! Come home!

Your legs tremble
under the weight of your visions.
Your heart is in overdrive.
Someone, please take my hand.

Come Egypt! Come Home!

Teresa E. Gallion

How can this be such a powerful plea
after four thousand plus years.
I know not the voice singing for me.
But I feel the purity and innocence
of the call from the temple walls.

Come Egypt! Come home!

Which one of you standing here with me
stained these temple walls with life colors
hear the call like a prayer?

Come Egypt! Come home!

Egyptian Yacht

Peace flows over me like a soothing melody.
My heart expands and love floods my bones.
Ecstasy makes me float like a goddess.

I cannot pull the words from my mouth
to capture the feelings invading my brain.
Perhaps silence is the best response
as I gaze at morning's light
streaking across the Nile River.

We float on an Egyptian yacht.
The Aida is forever imprinted on our hearts.
It gently carries us on this majestic river.

We are all at peace savoring the magic
in the quiet float on a powerful waterway
that transports the weight of humanity downstream.

The inner pictures of my soul
are not ready to release.
They tease me with no mercy.
I yield and bend my knees
on this sacred deck
in praise of this River.

Living in the moment is the key.
I savor the endless love
flowing through this morning
and hold my robust coffee
close to the chest.

Brief Exposure

The edge of evening
is the last exhale
of the sun on the horizon.

Orange cream
lays across the mountain peaks.
My eyes slant upward
to gaze at natural light.

Illusions of fire and ice
waiver in the twilight.
A frost-bitten wind
staggers to sleep.

The stars slowly roll out
on black velvet.
Happy yawns open wide
and my eyes fold in slumber.

Goddess of Protection

Egypt you live in my skin.
Soaking in the Nile River
rubbing off dead layers,
I feel you more intensely through time.

I walk like a goddess across the land
and claim this space as my domain.
I was here before all of you 21st century
walkers discovered my existence

preserved in the sands of time.
Eons of sunrises and sunsets
have graced this space.
Thousands of souls have worked

land by the river,
abused the sacred water
unable to destroy the spiritual flow.
I am the goddess of protection

who floats on a river wielding the power
of healing-water-bearer. Cleansing the water
of negative energy through eternity.

Teresa E. Gallion

Egyptian Moment

Handsome young 21st century Egyptian lad
greets us at the camel auction.
Stares with an amused smile
at the alien invasion of his land of birth.

We wave and wink at young innocence
as our auction experience ends
with the sale of many camels.

He chases us on his donkey as we bounce
in a truck bed with makeshift seats
down a dusty rode waving
in front of his angelic smile.

What will you be pretty-brown boy?
What will you be
when you become a man?

King and I

He is black velvet,
smooth as the midnight sky,
proud of his four-legged humpback
with a smile of ancient dignity.

He grants me the privilege
to ride his ship of the desert
in exchange for a few golden coins.

His camel's name is King.
King and the beautiful Nubian
escort me up the trail.

He is happy. King is happy.
I am ecstatic
riding this Nubian's camel
on sacred ancient land.

The beauty of these wonderful creatures
is their smile with heads held high.
I expose my joyful smile
in communion with King.

Nubian Prince

A Black velvet Nubian
walks into my line of sight.
I want to kiss his subtle lips
and delicately blended cheeks.

I look into his eyes
and say, you are beautiful.
I ask the translator to tell him.

His smile rains gratitude
on my heart as I float
in the ecstasy of the Blue Nile River.
My smile begins to glow as his radiates.

I bathe in the wonder of how
Black born again from the tombs
of a thousand years is so beautiful.

And I know at the next level.
I am blessed with the gaze
of a Nubian Prince.

Pinch me please.
My body is begging
for a reality check.
My soul is out of control.

Horse and Buggy Ride

A minaret in the Village of Esna
sounds the call to prayer.
I ride a buggy through
the crowded streets to
the Temple of Khnum.

A bustling crowd of humanity
from diverse cultures and nations
are going in the same direction
chasing the wind and waves of time.

We want to see the magnificence
of temples rising from the sand.
The intrigue of nature's power
to hold beauty and stories
after a few thousand treks around the sun.

The locals speed past in variable
modes of transport doing their daily tasks.
Some seek out the excited tourist
to loosen some change from their pockets.

Goddess in the Sahara

In the Sahara my soul swims
in ancient red sand.
I imagine a goddess rising
with the new dawn.

A healing goddess floats
in her light body across
a pure saturated blue expanse
above the sacred sand,
spreads her healing balm on earth.

The feminine energy engages in balance
with the earth touching human flesh.
Spirits rise from deep sleep.
Shake off the drought of inflamed sickness.

Together these Spirits
follow the goddess
in the road rover of healing
along the bay of trepidation,
to bring home the miserable
children of earth.

We must put them to sleep
to heal them and bring them
back to a new earth
in their next incarnation.

Homage to Aida Dehabeya

You embrace softly as we float
quietly against the gentle wind.
The timeless lyrical flow

of the Nile River is
a piece of heaven on earth
cuddling us in grace.

The bustling scenery unfolds with water buffalo,
donkeys, tuk-tuks, horse and buggy rides,
trucks, farmers tending their fields
and children running and waving.

I sing your name in morning's glow
filled with gratitude for the experience
of a true Egyptian yacht.

The smile on my face
tells a story of the sunset
on the river and my heart.

Aida Dehabeya!

Aida Dehabeya!

Habibi! Habibi!

Shapeshifting Between Time and Space

The soul travels daily
On the inner planes
Eating the knowledge given
With each invitation to dinner

Come Egypt

Reserved Space

The backend of the ax
beats stakes into the ground
to hold my tent in place next to the river.
Still, it is not secure.
The wind may take it away.

I do not want to be held in place
like this tent. I want to swim
deep and rise like a phoenix,
reborn as goddess of this river
singing in the choir of its flow.

I feel the heaviness of a thousand years
dragging me in my contemplative state.
I move forward by Divine Grace
on the Nile River and flood the landscape
to renew the earth.

Now I float in the Arkansas River
that gives pleasure to ungrateful humans.
For a moment, I still feel the Blue Nile
massaging all my senses.

I throw a kiss of gratitude at two rivers
and hold space in my heart.
I inhale the vigorous flow of the Arkansas River
and feel the Nile running through my veins.

Mount Nebo Reflections

Standing on top of Mount Nebo
surrounded by the strain of a sandstorm,
I cannot see the Dead Sea.

I see the Spirits of the Pharaohs,
images of their gods and goddesses
and I see Moses looking
into the Promised Land.

Souls on the color spectrum
parade across my visual bridge
from the ancient lands.

I feel confused until Spirit
brushes my face with wind currents
and my ears hear:

All my souls are broken
stroking massive egos,
drowning in pride
and bring material trash
to an afterlife that does not accept
gold nor silver charms.

Only light bodies may enter
the heavenly kingdoms.
We do not learn.
We still hold onto
the sorceress greed.

Against the Sun

Every time I hug a tree
I know the hug of Spirit.
I hold tight for a while
just to feel that energy.

I whisper into the bark,
thank you.
My ears hear,
you're welcome.
Go share your love.

And I think of you
floating down the Nile
holding my hand.
I catch my breath
one moment and you are gone.

I walk back into the present
and your blue-green eyes say,
not ready.
A tear drop rolls down your face.

You are still frozen in that past life
when we fought against the sun.

Come Egypt

The River Still Flows

My walking meditation draws me
to the Spirit of the Rio Grande,
soothing in the morning light.

I feel regal
after the benediction
of an Egyptian massage.

No words to adequately describe
the ancient hold of energy
of temple ruins and tombs

unearthed in all their glory
tease my many lifetimes
sitting here beside the river.

I am remarkably blessed
here in the Bosque
with a wave of New Mexico

love light surrounding me.
I gaze the eloquence
of delightful cottonwood

as it sings in green lyrics
all around the river and me.
I could shout my gratitude

over and over again
and that would not be sufficient
to express my joy

Teresa E. Gallion

to be home
in my beloved New Mexico
reflecting on my journey.

I touch the Rio Grande,
step out of my body
into the Nile River.

I feel the weight of 4000 years
speak to me in tongues
I can understand when it tells me:

I am still here.
Mankind may pollute and abuse me,
cause a temporary flu,
but cannot destroy me.

I will be here when
all the pathetic souls of earth
leave the planet
for I am eternal.

I am the key of life.
I am the fluid of life.
I am the Goddess of energy.
I will survive another 4000 years.
I will still be here.

My soul feels the cold vigor
of those years making me tremble
in the magnitude of these words.

It is the power of earth
to tell its story in generational waves

Come Egypt

as we repeat the cycles of life and death
and the river still flows.

Coming back to my body,
I sit by the Rio Grande,
run my fingers across the water.

Feel the connection between
the Nile River and the Rio Grande
in the essence of a River's flow.

Ancient Sightings

A songbird serenades my senses
in the Temple of Philae.
I want to fill the hollow space
in my heart with the embrace of Isis.

How can I be here and there
between my high desert home
and the desert of Egypt?
Shapeshifting like a hungry ghost,
I can trace hieroglyphics and petroglyphs
running back and forth
between divergent planes.

My breath releases a soul
riding on the fingertips of clouds
above the Valley of the Kings
and the Petroglyph National Monument.

The thunder of color rides
the ship of the desert and
I smile back at those fellows
strutting in the sand.
High top boots strut near my home.

Night approaches like a lost lover
and I am wired from Turkish coffee
screaming through my naked veins.
I must silence the thunder.

American cicadas and ancient
Egyptian scarabs sing loud

Come Egypt

in the summer heat of the valleys.
I want to trap this experience
like a clawing honeysuckle
and savor the exposure.

Hieroglyphics and Butterscotch

I drink from a cup with your imprint.
I ask the goddess on the mountain
if you are real.

She says swallow and digest the love
of angels swelling your belly.
Your angel wings will grow.

I take a sip and smile
like the camels in my dreamboat.
I am instantly transferred to Egypt.

I hug the walls of hieroglyphics
in Rameses II Temple at Abu Simbel
and feel a thousand moans call my name.

I close my eyes and hug a ponderosa tree,
smell butterscotch and vanilla bark.
A New Mexico Mountain massages my soul.

Water Lyrics

Waterfalls sing such beautiful lyrics.
Sit beside a sacred waterfall.
Close your eyes and absorb
the lyrics of nature's choir
serenade the soul, vibrate bones,
send tremors through veins.
Inhale the mist of bubbles
floating on air just a moment in time.
Rejuvenate the spirit and rise
born again in nature's embrace.

Now Egypt keeps intruding
on my waterfall dreams.
Ancient desert sand unveils
temples and tombs of a master civilization
that grabs, holds tight and speaks.
Listen to the lyrics on the walls.
They tell intimate stories thousands of years old.

Mind melding the ears of the present
overwhelm the senses.
An ancient history so powerful,
it is difficult for 21st century homo sapiens
to breathe in and assimilate.

The mind tries to pull away
from this intensity.
Floats back to its waterfall dreams
flowing into the Nile River
and the Rio Grande.

River Fantasy

The river rises reaching for sky
like an eagle soaring and my third eye
opens to embrace bliss.

All I need to do is float in this river of light.
Hovering on the Nile River
with sparkles of blue so intense,

I feel the vibrations of your love.
Thousands of miles across the ocean,
my body moves in harmony with you.

When the light begins to fade
I will carry you through the storms.
When the sun rises above the mountain,

you will be next to me, holding my hand,
laying your head on my chest.
We will savor the morning light.

United in joyfulness,
will it be here on the Yacht or sitting
by the Rio Grande?

Waking Dream

I hear your voice on the inner planes.
It massages my soul with your love potions.
I release my love in the wind.
You catch it in the center of your heart.

There on the deck of Aida
I see you swimming in the Nile River.
The blue water embraces your body.

You are such a tease and I cannot swim.
I lay my head back on the deck chair,
close my eyes, imagine myself floating
with you in the river.

I know I am flirting in a waking dream.
Cloud surfing above the river
watching us float downstream.

New Mexico blesses me with sassy clouds.
Allows me to surf on fluffy trails,
climb white mountains,
and hug clouds above the desert sand.

Cloud surfing is a remarkable experience
shapeshifting between the Egyptian desert
and New Mexico's enchanted land.
I float in gratitude on the waves of clouds.

Pathway to Growth

I open the window to my soul
and am amazed at all the beauty
peacefully, patiently, pondering
in my garden waiting for me
to step in and touch the love rose.

The purple wave of heaven spins
magical charms along the highway.
Follow the magic lines
in the streaming light.

Ancient Egyptian gods and goddesses
play in my garden and tempt me to
ride the wave of the ancient ones.
I cannot go backwards to repeat
the woes of any ancient history.

I must go forward into the light.
The pathway to growth is there.

Come Egypt

Abu Simbel Intrusion

Night frost brings
the soothing balm
of light and sound
rippling past camp.

Sleepy eyes fold.
Dreams come and escort you
to the secret garden.

Here you may sit in peace.
Absorb the wisdom
of violets, paintbrush, and daisies.

You may bow in reverence
to a mushroom's
artistic expression.

Now feel the music
of a wild blade of grass
sing close to your legs.

You were born to taste beauty
and hold space for the broken.
Come hither and sleep with me.

But I cannot sleep with you dear nature
for the pull of the river Nile is teasing me
and the Temple of Abu Simbel calls my name.

After 3000 years, his ego still echoes
in the desert wind. One hundred wives have stood
at his foot and cursed his hand against the breast.

Teresa E. Gallion

How many times have you come back here,
Rameses II, in the last 3000 years and longed
to assert your authority on the sacred feminine?

You dominate the ancient landscape
rising from the sand at Luxor.
Your ego explodes at the Luxor temple.

The sheer size of your monuments
raise the question about your worship of deities.
Were you really paying tribute to Amun-Ra?

I cannot sleep with nature tonight.
Your hold is too tight.
Let go Rameses, let go.

Woman of Value

If the Egyptians had not denied Nefertiti
as a possible pharaoh, we might have missed
the calligraphy that tells her story
from walls of ancient ruins.
She still intrigues in the 21st century.

I feel good in my retirement
as I stretch beyond my comfort zone,
discover the inner bliss of conquering fear.
Like Nefertiti, I am powerful
and it flows from deep within.

I am made from the experiences
of many lifetimes, recognize
so much progress on my journey,
feel my own inner strength
and know freedom like an eagle in flight.

My season to blossom awakens my spirit.
I face the forest, smile and
trees wink at me in admiration.
My heart swells with gratitude
for blessings that float in my river of light.

My garden bears fruit
from many years of toil, labor,
sweat, rejection, pain and suffering.
I rise strong from negative ashes,
drift in ecstatic radiance
with the vigor of a woman of value.

Egyptian Portal

You slip behind bushes sheltering my garden.
The soil speaks to you in an ancient dialect.
A powerful vibration makes your legs tremble
and lose the ability to hold you up.

Your mouth tries to ask who speaks
to you with such gentle but forceful authority
and hold your ears prisoners here and now.

You want to back away from the vibrations.
You find your body is frozen in the moment.
Surrender is the only option and you just listen.

You think of a song, this is your house.
A holy house of prayer where the seeker cometh
before the sacred land of nature.
Knees bend in humility and receive
the wisdom pulsating from earth.

A reminder, even in ancient Egypt,
we are simply souls passing through.
May we learn to walk with
grace, gratitude, compassion and love.

Come Egypt

Musings on the Nile River

The muse speaks to the river
When it pleases her
Sends messages of love
To those able to hear

Come Egypt

Words to Love You

I want these words to love you.
I scroll them across the page,
an offering to the universe
for all ears able to receive.

Because

I want these words to love you,
lift you up in times of distress,
push you forward when you want
to run away from the challenge.

Because

I want these words to love you
when you freeze at the gates of fear,
and push you through with
the heat of love in each syllable.

Because

I want these words to love you,
squeeze the impurity from your veins
to help you walk lightly
on your journey against the wind.

Because

I want these words to love you,
keep you eternally warm,
rub your legs with stamina
to carry you through the storm.

Come Egypt

Because

I want these words to love you
and bring you to me.
I am dancing on the river Nile
waiting to capture your smile.

Because

I love you.

Teresa E. Gallion

Scream into the Silence

Entwined in the sound of your voice,
I am trapped.
I hug a tree for life
and try not to drown in your hold.
My body tries to take leave of you.
My mind and Soul do not want to let go.

I breathe out and flowers bloom
around me. You ambushed me
with the sound floating from your tongue.
A soothing speakeasy manipulates my senses.
Your cold tracks linger in my brain.
Word Slayer!
Songs of remembering play in my head.

I run through the catacombs of time.
You flirt ahead just far enough
to keep me chasing your light
lifetime after lifetime.

Thoughts of you become a benediction
and winter feels long in the desert
as you dance in the sand
against a blue nautical sky.

My heart skips a beat with each breath.
I scream into the silence.

Waiting for You

You speak to me in a language
that only you and I understand.
You embrace with words
longing to touch, but afraid to reach.

I sing soft lyrics that vibrate in your soul.
You hug them gently because you feel love
that has yet to be acknowledged in your loins.

The air is giving birth to seedlings
to germinate in your garden.
Each is a blessing engraved in your name.

You cannot sleep at night
and you know not why.
It is because your soul is restless
and wants to come to me
where love waits for you
in the eternal garden.

Soul Upheaval

Just a thought of you
makes me wet with desire.
I want to pull my heart out

and serve it to you on a gold platter.
My Soul says, no you cannot.
No one is worthy of such sacrifice.

The silent landscape of my brain
is sweating with fever,
pulsating with fear.

Flames of healing lick me red
with untouchable love.
Do you dare approach?

Only those able to walk barefoot
in my garden
avoid the kiss of the thorn.

The petal of the rose
wraps the goodhearted
in the garden.

Thorns bleed the unworthy,
bury them deep
in darkness.

Catch the Wave

The open road is the only opium
you need to experience freedom
trembling in your luscious body.

Ride your rubber wheels on asphalt
and throw kisses to the clouds.
They will speak back to you
in rainbows and water blossoms.

Look, listen and savor every love stimulus
riding the open road beside you.
The sky is falling for you.
Embrace the gift with love notes.

A low rider in the desert
on a highway to nowhere
seeks the still solitude
of desert spaces that call spirit home.

No need to worry about
the distance nor danger.
The desert holds the keys
to your life. Each key
is given when readiness is achieved.

Do not forget to lookup.
The clouds stream messages
just for your eyes.
Be vigilant and catch the wave.

Law of Silence

Silence is a golden treasure chest
in the city of subtle wisdom.
I still have miles to go to get there.
Those single silent coins tease me.

I reflect on the Law of Silence
and the chatter of self-talk
becomes a wave of calmness.
I am learning to remain still
in the long lean into maturity.

I have traveled the noisy road,
learned soft surrender.
The beauty of that concept
opens me to join the silence
of the light shining through.
I discover the remedy
for healing resides within me.

Lyrical Release

Sacred syllables ride up my spine
create a flash flood in my brain.
Raging ripples spit wild words.

I want to catch and release
soft baked words of wisdom,
ride sea waves,
float down rivers,
climb mountains and see the world
as a lake of goodness.

I want to mute all voices
and massage faces
with lyrical phrases
that move mountains to shiver,
grass to sway in open meadows,
rocks to slide down hillsides.

When the sound current of love
slaps me in the face,
may my arms open
and receive sacred lyrics.

Soar Like an Eagle

Waves dance for me today.
What a flamboyant flirt.
But I cannot follow them out to sea.
It is not my time to walk on water.

Spirits encircle me.
Tell me to step back, enjoy the view.
Let sand massage my feet.

Time sits on every horizon,
will be there for you
in the appropriate season.

Go forth, enjoy nature's offerings.
Your respect for dear Mother
has earned you a rite of passage
into her beautiful places.

You may soar like an eagle
across Mother's land.
Grab her love streams
caressing you in sacred wind.

Never Alone Again

I come from the womb of love.
Open to embrace a soaring heart
riding on wind battered time.

The sacred dead rest beneath sand
and rub my eyes on bygone ages. I am
drunk on ancient water rolling over my breast.

My bones are a temple of love
that rose from the pure elixir of the Nile.
I bath in sacred water and wait

for you to write hieroglyphics
of love on the walls of my body
and massage my bloodstream.

I want to join my flow to yours forever,
float in the essence of pure light.
Never leave me alone again.

Redemption

Take your eyes to the tears' laundry.
Wash them well. Go back on deck.
See the world in a new light.

Blood streams down your face.
I want to touch you but know
I cannot expose what is forbidden.

You are an image of me
in the window of my past lives
floating down the Nile.

The marriage of water and light
pulls me close to the river.
I want to touch purity in that union,
but cannot bear to embrace it.

The memory is too painful.
Perhaps next time when
the scar feels less tender.

My desires stand in shadows
stoking fires burning inside me
working to expand my fears.

Now, I understand the gift of stubbornness.
I shall not be ruled by fear.
Goddess of the river smiles
as we ride currents celebrating my insight.

Come Egypt

Temple Hopping – Tomb Walking

A woman went into the desert broken
The temples and tombs massaged her soul
She returned to face humankind
As a goddess of healing and love

Come Egypt

Teresa E. Gallion

My Womb

My womb lies beneath blackberries
in an unknown country
where no one sings without permission.
Threat of demise is a lethal weapon
for unwanted gestures.

My womb is surrounded by red roses
that moisturize stems at
a mere thought of you.
Such power is dangerous
for the untried who dare
to take what is not given.

My womb is standard bearer,
holds the diamonds to expand the world,
trained to submit to gods
and bear fruit for the common man.

My womb is a goddess
reserved for the gods
of compassion and love.
Do not come to me
with blood-stained negative bouquets.

My womb is the sacred feminine
open to the flow of love
streaming through sand
climbing on stones of delight.

My womb is a kingdom
of hieroglyphic walls holding
their breath as diggers reach

Come Egypt

into ecstatic bliss of sand
preserving my essence.

My womb is an empire beneath sand.
Those curious humans unearth my glory.
They may bleed me dry someday
with the profiteer's greed and lust.

Teresa E. Gallion

Dear Nefertari

You stand out in my memory bank.
Even ancient Greeks paid homage
to your beautiful prowess
and intellectual power.
They gave you gifts of silver that stood out
against all the gold adorning your body.

Your tomb is a womb of majesty.
Were you surprised to find out
when your soul left the body,
you could not take any trinkets
with you into your next life?

After 3000 years your tomb
rose from the sand.
You left a legacy of feminine power
that screamed into the future.
Many stand before your beautiful
imagery in awe. Some read
hieroglyphics that sing your story.

Many gods are depicted in your tomb.
Your presence is a power symbol
of feminine energy given
from the heavenly planes.

Or was it simply Rameses II glorifying
his most beloved of many females?
He was busy but always found his way
back to your arms.
He took your body but never conquered
your soul.

Come Egypt

How many times have you returned to earth
to fight for freedom of the sacred feminine?
How many times have you stood on the edge
of our planet overwhelmed with sacred water
flowing from your eyes to bathe the sadness
nature holds?

What Bodies

Did someone put up a for sale sign
on sand buried tombs with an asking price
no one could fold arms around?

The mummies of the Pharaohs
pulled from their tombs tremble
for the souls that left them
thousands of years ago.
Subjected to the hawk eyes
of curious humans, there is
nothing to save them.

What bodies do those Pharaohs
possess in the 21st century?
Do they feel the pain of ages
when they look at the bodies
left so long ago?

Did they participate in the unearthing
of tombs to discover their old bodies?
Or did they become Egyptologists
in today's historic arena fascinated
by the past lives they may not recognize?

We know the concept of digging
is also a human concept like other animals.
It's called curiosity sometimes peppered
with greed in humankind.

Key of Life

Every tomb I enter
the Key of Life stares
at me from sacred carvings.

I rub words on the wall.
A window opens and I see
chariots of lifetime after lifetime pass by.
The master's whip scars horses
and they run without a destiny.

The hieroglyphics roll across my skin.
Awakening my sensors to light
bearers of a thousand years.
I drink deep into the past,
see intellectual vibrancy
and darkness sucking on dry bones.

Today light and darkness
still rides wind across the planet.
We adjust to ugly, sip indifference,
bathe in numbness and freeze kindness.

Suddenly the window closes.
A strong feeling of déjà vu
binds me to the imagery.

The key of life is eternal
and opens and closes gates
like an unending wave.

Teresa E. Gallion

Dancing in the Valley of the Kings

The last word ran across velvet night.
A pen clings to blank space on her papyrus
as sleep captures her under the stars.
Dragon light is born every morning she exhales.

Wilted collard greens tickle the tongue.
Cornbread crumbs paint the chest.
Thoughts of faraway places
mingle with her digestion.

She holds pain in a spare tire.
No flats allowed today.
The rough road rocks the rubber
carrying her forward.

She bounces with the rolling wheels
on a mission to seek and find her way home.
Sunrise winks at her.
With respect, she smiles in the color of gratitude.

A brake for a nap and dreams takeover.
She strolls down the Valley of the Kings.
Did you know Pharaohs and Queens
dance at night with gods and goddesses

when all the people walkers go home?
The tourist does not know about this nightly fling.
Comparing notes from tomb to tomb,
a disappointing discovery is made.

Come Egypt

None of the gold and trinkets
can dance in the light.
Useless they are to light bodies
dancing throughout the night.

Letter to Tutankhamun

Dear Tut,
Have you passed by lately?
Did you notice people
staring at your mummy
in awe and amazement
of the power of preservation
in a grain of sand.

I stopped by today and
scanned the walls of your tomb,
turned away from the intensity
of your mummy.
The monkeys on your tomb wall
lightened things up.

I wonder if you had a sense of humor.

Hatshepsut

History tells me you were one of the greatest
female rulers in world history.
You had to hide your womanhood
to rule a massive kingdom.

Female Pharaoh of the 18th Dynasty,
we stand and admire the spectacular
presence of your temple risen from sand.
A showcase of magnificence to glorify you.

Your shrine competes in grandeur
with Rameses II at Abu Simbel.
All mouths open in awe as they approach
an elegant walk to the entrance.

I feel your regal presence watching
pilgrims pay homage to your reign.
Your smile of knowingness from the hilltop
exposes the power of feminine energy.

I press my feet on your temple floor
and feel your energy saying,
I am Hatshepsut, Pharaoh of Egypt.
Walk with humility and respect in my sanctuary.

It Was a Lie

Touch me gently.
My scars run deep and tender.
That's what she hears as her fingers
caress hieroglyphics on the wall
to connect to a thousand
years frozen in time.

The story on the wall speaks of treasures.
The sarcophagus is barren
and the room is empty.
Disappointment trolls in the tomb.

She speaks to the lingering Soul
crouched in the corner
waiting for deliverance.
Take my hand friend.
It was a lie.
You cannot take anything
with you to the afterlife.

Goddess Isis Speaks

I have taken you in everyway
a goddess can.
The fruit of my labor bursts
between my legs.
Feminine power bleeds down my thighs.

You are caught in the awe
of my power.
I suckle you at will
until my thirst is quenched.

Then I lay you gently upon earth
and tell my story of conqueror
on these walls with the art of my pen.

One day I will return to this temple,
behold the beauty of the goddess hands
that scrolled on these walls.

I will stroll across the temple walls
and wander in awe.
Who bequeathed this beauty
risen from sand?

Teresa E. Gallion

Descendant Ones

I am water and you are fire sucking me up.
Someday, I will dry up or you will burn out.
Either way, we win in the balance of nature.

The only way to rise again is from the ashes
or dried sand cleaned to begin anew
an unspoken vow to live as kings and queens.

Was that your intention descendant ones,
to hail an afterlife as ornate as ancient Egypt?

I sing to silence a thanksgiving prayer.
Life goes on even after I leave
and earth renews itself.

I pay homage to all the trinkets you left
in your tombs dearly beloved ones.
Which one was for me, I do not know.

I am happy to walk this piece of earth again
knowing I do not need to take anything with me
when I cross the rainbow bridge.

Light of love will open its door
and that is enough to sustain me.
I will come back and try again
to learn to love and be of service.

I walk these tombs today in remembrance.
I hear a melodious cry
of an ancient Egyptian phoenix
serenading my inner solitude.

Come Egypt

I hear a dialect only my heart understands.
It is singing the stories of many lifetimes
of a glorious civilization inscribed in time.

Confused, yet pulled by energy
of this space called Egypt.
The power of its purpose continues unfolding
as archaeologists still dig daily.

One obsessed generation after another
attempts to decipher the power
of a regal civilization.

Every new dig tempts souls to return,
to see, to hear, the noise of ancient ones
rise from the sand.

Teresa E. Gallion

Behold Me

A Nightingale sits on the foot of Rameses III.
He stares beyond my physical body.
No outward sound comes from his throat.

Yet I feel the engaging deep lyrics within.
It is a welcome song to enter the tomb.

I feel an empathetic body
lean against my light body
with the scent of love
rolling from eyes that see through me.

What is the message for me
as I enter this tomb greeted with hello.

My spiritual wings open
and light flows through me.
The intensity of the message
floats across the tomb's wall.
Welcome dearly beloved.

How has your journey progressed
the last three thousand years?
Let us talk. I want to behold
your magnificent spirit shining through.

Ancient Myths of the Gods

Out of a universe of chaos,
sun god Ra reaches for sky and
floats to the underworld every evening

as light sheds from daylight
in a spectacular showcase of sunset.
Endless cycles of life and death

akin to a phoenix burning
and rising from its ashes.
A story is woven and lies dormant

below earth surface through centuries.
A new generation stretches in awe
of what continues to rise from sand.

The sun god Ra continues to rise in the sky
and float to the underworld every evening.
Souls of humankind

are still intrigued by writings
on temple walls telling a story
of ancient Egyptian myths and deities.

Wall Paintings

I love it when walls talk.
The soft sensual paintings
pull at my cleavage
and rough rugged edges slap hard.

These ruins gifted from the desert sand
are poetry to my soul.
I ask fairies of the universe
to take me for a ride
on the scales of these walls.
Imprint me with hieroglyphics
that burn with the golden tongue wisdom
my soul needs.

The wall paintings shackled in the sand
have been waiting four thousand plus one year
for humble souls ready to eat
the knowledge painted on the walls.

When the fairies pause in midflight
I see a mirror image of myself
dressed like a queen who smiles at me.

Inhale and Exhale

Between inhale and exhale,
I make love to you dear Egypt.
A thousand times died and risen

like a sun goddess from the Nile River
to watch your royal legacy unfold
through millennia.

You hold the Nile as a moist blanket.
The river has been a faithful servant
and still flows like a quiet powerful storm.

Every drop has a first and last word.
Music flows from the river
with no end to harmony.

I stand here on the deck of Aida
and see visions of temples and tombs
waiting to be discovered.

I sing praise to a river
that survives under the onslaught
of a human invasion over time.

Hallelujah Egypt

Sometimes there are things
that cannot be captured
in words nor pictures.

They must be simply experienced.
That is the glory of ancient Egypt.
That is the power of preservation.

Standing before such splendor
is beyond words.
Seeing and feeling smacks
at the core of the spirit
and defies description.

Even hallelujah is not
a sufficient response.
Witness the artistic vigor of a majestic
civilization as it embraces the senses.

Just bow your head in humility.

Come Egypt

Epilogue

About the Author

Teresa E. Gallion was born in Shreveport, Louisiana and moved to Illinois at the age of 15. She completed her undergraduate training at the University of Illinois Chicago and received her master's degree in Psychology from Bowling Green State University in Ohio. She retired from New Mexico state government in 2012.

She moved to New Mexico in 1987. While writing sporadically for many years, in 1998 she started reading her work in the local Albuquerque poetry community. She has been a featured reader at local coffee houses, bookstores, art galleries, museums, libraries, Outpost Performance Space, the Route 66 Festival in 2001, the State of Oklahoma's Poetry Festival in Cheyenne, Oklahoma in 2004 and the New Mexico Poetry Summit 2023.

Teresa's work is published in numerous Journals and anthologies. She has two CDs: *On the Wings of the Wind* and *Poems from Chasing Light*. She has published four books: *Walking Sacred Ground, Contemplation in the High Desert, Chasing Light* and *Scent of Love*.

Chasing Light was a finalist in the 2013 New Mexico/Arizona Book Awards.

Scent of Love was a finalist in the 2021 New Mexico/Arizona Book Awards.

Teresa is blessed to live in a high desert sanctuary where the sun shines more than 325 days a year, the blue vaulted sky sports the most spectacular clouds and the night sky twinkles with ecstatic brilliance. Add to that the indescribably beautiful New Mexico landscape that draws artist and writers from all over the world. Within that context, she often finds her head in the clouds whether walking the city streets, a desert arroyo or a Ponderosa Pine trail. For her, the New Mexico landscape is sacred ground for a poet to write. She is blessed to share this space with the souls of Rumi and Hafiz (both Persian mystic poets) on quiet walks in the desert and mountains that stimulate the creative flow.

Teresa is a seeker working on unfolding spiritually in this present lifetime. When she is not writing, she is committed to traveling the world and hiking the enchanted landscapes of New Mexico.

You may preview her work at
http://teresagallion.yolasite.com

About Mary Dezember

Jason Collin Photography

Mary Dezember creates stories and poetry as portals to possibilities. She states: "We spell words and, arranged well, words can put a spell on us." Her novel and her two books of poetry explore the rite of passage to identity, including the hero's emotional and intellectual quest. She earned her Ph.D. in Comparative Literature from Indiana University. Professor Emeritus of English at New Mexico Tech, she is an advocate of creativity. Mary finds the magic of life by channeling the muse or reading a good book. She lives in the Land of Enchantment. Her website is marydezember.com.

What People are Saying

Debbi Brody conducts poetry workshops and readings throughout the USA to writers age five through ninety-five. She publishes frequently in regional and national and international literary journals and anthologies. Her first collection, "Portraits in Poetry," (Village Books Press, Oklahoma, 2006), as well as her chapbook," FreeForm" are out of print. Her recent chapbooks, "Awe in the Muddle", "Walking the Arroyo" and her 2015 collection "In Everything Birds," (Village Books Press, Oklahoma, 2015) are available through artqueen58@aol.com . She has returned to Decatur, Illinois for retirement and has completed a tween fantasy novel due out in late 2024.

Only the voice of a mature poet can summon the beauty and strength of image and spirit as thoroughly as Teresa Gallion in her 5th full length poetry collection. She crosses literal and metaphoric rivers and deserts through time and space helping the reader understand the many ways these places and people are all connected. And isn't connection what the well lived life is about? Connecting with this book feels timeless while simultaneously brings the illusive present moment in focus, the one that's hard to grasp and the best place to be. Although this volume is so rich it could be an apex in her life's work, I sincerely hope to read at least another book spoken from her soul.

Debbi Brody

Poet and Writer

Kim is a retired Visual Effects Producer (Twister, Saving Private Ryan, Galaxy Quest) who now write plays, acts and directs live theater in Northern California. An ardent reader of literature, poetry and non-fiction, a travel enthusiast and rescuer of dogs and cats, Kim splits her time as evenly as possible between these beloved pursuits. Her travels in Egypt left her breathless and longing for more. To follow Kim's theatrical pursuits go to kimbromley.com or follow her on Instagram at kbromley57.

Teresa Gallion beautifully captures the raptures of historical and present day Egypt and all it evokes both in real life and in lore. Fellow travelers, whether through life, time or Egypt itself will be tugged by the imagery and emotion of connection to the earth, our history and our humanity. Having experienced Egypt alongside Teresa, I was moved by the flood of memories and by the insight into Teresa's deeply felt experiences and sensations of an adventure we both longed for and finally embraced with all our hearts.

Kim Bromley

Writer/Actor/Fellow Traveler

Kim Ports Parsons grew up near Baltimore, earned degrees, and worked as an educator and librarian for thirty years. Now she lives near Shenandoah National Park, writes, gardens, walks, and volunteers for Cultivating Voices LIVE Poetry. Her poems appear in many print and online publications, including Skylight 47, LIVE ENCOUNTERS, Poetry Ireland Review and Vox Populi and have been nominated for a Pushcart. Her first collection, The Mayapple Forest (Terrapin Books 2022), was a finalist for the North American Book Award, a national competition sponsored by the Poetry Society of Virginia.

Visit her at : www.KimPortsParsons.com.

"I sing your name in morning's light," Teresa Gallion declares to the ancient land and civilization she celebrates, in poems of ecstasy and awe, in her new collection, *Come Egypt*. The poet writes "words to spell grace," as she describes her experiences of spiritual connection, mystery, and revelation, inspired by her travels through the countryside and historical sites. Vivid scenes are evoked for the reader; "A minaret in the Village of Esna/ sounds the call to prayer," and a "camel: ship of the desert" delights the speaker as she rides. Gallion's passionate voice threads its way through this reverent collection, declaring "Egypt is... the goddess of protection/ who floats on the river."

Kim Ports Parsons

author *The Mayapple Forest*
(Terrapin Books 2022)

Dr. Michael Anthony Ingram is a retired professor and poet. He taught Counselor Education and Supervision at Oregon State University. He founded the DC Poetry Project, Inc. and hosts the Quintessential Listening: Poetry Online Radio and YouTube podcast (www.qlporyt.com). He uses poetry to address issues of power and oppression, gaining global recognition. He travels widely, leading workshops on developing empathy skills through poetry. He was nominated for a Pushcart Prize and is working on a new poetry collection, "When Cherry Blossoms Fall on Black Skin." He lives in Washington, DC, where he blends poetry, activism, and mental health.

Embark on a mesmerizing journey through Teresa Gallion's poetry collection, "Come Egypt." Like a poetic travel guide for the mind, body, and soul, Teresa's adroit use of lyrical language transports readers to the front of pyramids, the banks of the Nile River, and aboard royal yachts. Each poem, soaked in vivid descriptors, invites you to join this captivating expedition.

In the opening poem, "Come Egypt," readers are beckoned to a poignant journey: "All my dreams spill over the waterfall. I watch the blossoms stream down. I see tombs of gods, goddesses, pharaohs beckoning my soul to come home." Teresa creatively covers terrain, as a reader I ride alongside her as she recalls trips to pyramids, ancient tombs, and shares stories of almost 4000-year-old queens from ancient Egypt.

Notably, queens like Nefertiti and Hatshepsut are etched in the pantheon of feminine greatness through Teresa's poignant and powerful poems. "A Woman of Value" honors Nefertiti, echoing lines such as, "Like Nefertiti, I am powerful and flow from within me." The overarching theme explores the power women possess individually and collectively.

In the poem "Goddess of the Sahara," asserts, "The feminine energy engages in balance with the earth touching human flesh." It illustrates the wholeness of the female world, where the sacred feminine is freed from convention and embraces the journey to self-discovery. Humor, intimacy, and desire are also prominent themes in the collection. Playful descriptions of men, such as the camel rider in "The King and I," evoke joyous laughter, while "River Fantasy" explores the belief that love transcends space, place, and time.

Teresa's words resonate as strong, proud, and luxurious, akin to the golden era of Luxor. The poem "Soar Like an Eagle" aptly describes her triumphant collection, celebrating the sacred feminine, the strength, and resilience of women, from commoners to queens. "Come Egypt" stands as a testament to Teresa's prowess as an incomparable wordsmith, offering readers a poetic odyssey that cherishes love, resilience, and the sacred feminine.

Dr. Michael Anthony Ingram

Host and Producer
Quintessential Listening:
Poetry Online Radio and YouTube (qlporyt.com)

Other Books

by

Teresa E. Gallion

~ * ~

Contemplation in the High Desert

Chasing Light

Scent of Love

~ * ~

All volumes are available at :

www.innerchildpress.com/teresa-e-gallion

www.teresagallion.yolasite.com
&
other fine book outlets

Inner Child Press

Inner Child Press is a publishing company founded and operated by writers. Our personal publishing experiences provide us an intimate understanding of the sometimes-daunting challenges writers, new and seasoned may face in the business of publishing and marketing their creative "Written Work".

For more information:

Inner Child Press

www.innerchildpress.com

intouch@innerchildpress.com

'building bridges of cultural understanding'

202 Wiltree Court, State College, Pennsylvania 16801

www.ingramcontent.com/pod-product-compliance
Lightning Source LLC
LaVergne TN
LVHW051845080426
835512LV00018B/3086